DISCOVERING Space

THE MOON

Ian Graham

W
FRANKLIN WATTS

An Appleseed Editions book

First published in 2007 by Franklin Watts

Franklin Watts
338 Euston Road, London NW1 3BH

Franklin Watts Australia
Level 17/207 Kent St, Sydney, NSW 2000

© 2007 Appleseed Editions

Appleseed Editions Ltd
Well House, Friars Hill, Guestling, East Sussex TN35 4ET

Created by Q2A Media
Series Editor: Honor Head
Designers: Diksha Khatri, Ashita Murgai
Picture Researchers: Lalit Dalal, Jyoti Sachdev

ISBN   978 0 7496 7546 2

Dewey classification: 523.3

All words in **bold** can be found in the glossary on page 30.

A CIP catalogue for this book is available from the British Library.

Picture credits
t=top b=bottom c=centre l=left r=right, m: middle
Cover images: Alaska Stock Images/ Photolibrary,
Small images: NASA: ml, Tunc Tezel: mr, Jet Propulsion Laboratory/ NASA: mc
Carolina K. Smith, M.D/ Shutterstock: Half title, Marbo: para head, Courtesy NASA/JPL-Caltech: 4b, 15br, Simcoe Skies
Astronomy: 5t, Index Stock Imagery/ Photolibrary: 5b, Alaska Stock Images/ Photolibrary: 6b, Doug Wilson/Corbis: 7t, Corbis: 7b,
Sergey Korotkih/ Shutterstock: 8b, Archivo Iconografico, S.A./ Corbis: 9l, Bettmann/Corbis: 9r, Johnson Space Center/ NASA Neil
A. Armstrong: 10b, Johnson Space Center/ NASA Eugene Cernan: 11t, Pacific Stock/ Photolibrary: 11b, Science Photo Library/
Photolibrary: 12-13 (background), 13b, Visuals Unlimited/ Corbis: 12b, Jim Craigmyle/ Corbis: 14bl, Roger Ressmeyer/
Corbis: 14-15 (background), 15bl, Apollo 17 Crew, NASA: 16b, Jet Propulsion Laboratory/ NASA: 17tl, Joe Huber: 17tr, NASA:
18b, 19t, 22b, 23b, 24b, Science Photo Library/ Photolibrary:19 (background), NASA Ames Research Center: 20b, Johnson Space
Center/ NASA Alan L. Bean: 21b, Johnson Space Center/ NASA Harrison Schmitt: 22-23 (background), Photo Researchers, Inc./
Photolibrary: 24-25 (background), NASA/ John Frassanito and Associates: 26b, 27b.

Printed in China

Franklin Watts is a division of Hachette Children's Books

Contents

The Moon 4

The Moon and water 6

Myth and magic 8

Moon rock 10

Waxing and waning 12

Moon studies 14

Rock and dust 16

The far side 18

Visiting the Moon 20

Moon walks 22

Eclipses 24

The future 26

Timeline 28

Glossary 30

Index 32

The Moon

Some planets have many moons, but the Earth has only one **moon**, called the Moon. The Moon is closer to Earth than anything else in the **Solar System**. At night, it is the biggest object we can see in the sky.

Ball of rock

The Moon is smaller than the Earth, but it is still a large object. It is a 73 billion billion tonne ball of rock. It is dry and dusty and covered with **craters**. It is so big and so close to the Earth that on a clear night we can easily see the marks on its surface.

The Moon spins as it travels around the Earth, so the same side of the Moon is always facing towards the Earth.

Spotlight on space

The Moon is the brightest object in the night sky, but it gives out no light of its own. It looks so bright because it is lit up by the Sun.

There are never any clouds on the Moon because the Moon has no **atmosphere**.

Sunlight bouncing off the Moon takes just over a second to travel to the Earth.

Man on the Moon

The way people think about the Moon has changed over the centuries. At first people thought it was a god or goddess. Later, some people believed it was like Earth with living things and cities. Eventually, scientists discovered that it is a rocky world without life. Now that **astronauts** have landed on the Moon and brought pieces of Moon rock back to Earth, we know a lot more about it.

The Moon and water

The Moon has seas, but no water. At first, scientists thought the big, dark areas of the Moon were seas. They are still called seas today even though we know they were never full of water. These are places where hot, liquid rock once flowed across the Moon.

Big and fast

The Earth's Moon is big compared with the dozens of moons that **orbit** other **planets**. It is the fifth biggest moon in the Solar System. It travels around the Earth at a speed of about 3,683 kph. That is about four times the speed of a jet airliner.

The word 'month' is named after the Moon, because the Moon takes about one month to go around the Earth.

Moon facts

Distance	▶	384,400 kilometres from Earth
Size across the middle	▶	3,476 million kilometres
Mass	▶	73 billion billion tonnes
Coldest part	▶	−173 degrees Celsius
Hottest part	▶	125 degrees Celsius

Spotlight on
space

The Moon is smaller than the Earth, so the pull of its gravity is weaker. If you were on the Moon you would weigh less so you would be able to jump higher and for longer distances.

The Moon's **gravity** causes the ocean tides on Earth.

High and low tides

The sea rises and falls around the world twice a day. These changes in sea levels are called **tides**. The tides are caused by the Moon pulling the water towards it and the Earth pulling the water back again. When the tide is out, we can see lots of beach and the sea looks far away. This is called low tide. When the tide is in, the water covers the beach. This is high tide.

Although the Moon is next to the Earth, it looks completely different. Its rough, rocky surface is lifeless and unchanging.

Myth and magic

In the ancient world, people thought the Moon was a god or goddess. Later, some scientists believed that moonlight could cause illness or even madness. In Latin, the language of ancient Rome, the word for moon is *luna*. That is where our word lunacy, meaning madness, comes from.

Howling at the Moon

Werewolves appear in **legends** about the Moon. They were said to be people who changed into wolves during the full Moon. They would snarl and howl and attack humans and other animals. As soon as the full Moon waned, they changed back into humans.

People thought that werewolves howled at the Moon when they changed from being a human into a wolf.

Names of Moon gods

Place	Name
Ancient Egypt ▶	Khons and Thoth
Ancient Greece ▶	Selene
Ancient Rome ▶	Luna
Hindu (India) ▶	Soma

Moon gods and goddesses

Ancient myths are full of stories about Moon gods. In Greek myths, the Moon goddess, Selene, came down to Earth every night to kiss a sleeping shepherd boy called Endymion. In ancient **Norse myths**, the Moon god, Mani, pulled the Moon across the sky while being chased by a wolf.

Diana was the ancient Roman goddess of the Moon and of hunting.

Spotlight on
space

In the days when no one knew whether people lived on the Moon, astronomers sometimes thought they saw signs of life there. In 1824, a German astronomer thought he could see cities on the Moon.

Early films showed people travelling to the Moon in search of Moon people.

Moon rock

Soon after the Earth formed, an object the size of a small planet crashed into it. The crash threw lots of rock into space. The pieces collected together, pulled in by their own gravity. The clump of rock grew and grew until it formed the Moon.

Inside the Moon

Moon's Crust ▶	70 kilometres thick on the side facing Earth
	150 kilometres thick on the far side
Mantle ▶	1,290 kilometres deep
Core ▶	680 kilometres across

Instruments placed on the Moon by astronauts let scientists measure the distance between the Earth and the Moon very accurately.

Flying away

The Moon has a small metal **core** surrounded by a layer of rock called the **mantle**, with a thin **crust** of rock on the outside. When it first formed, the Moon was ten times closer to the Earth than it is today. Since then, it has been slowly drifting away from Earth. Every year, it moves nearly four centimetres further away.

From Earth to Moon

No one was sure how the Moon formed until astronauts brought some Moon rocks back to Earth. The rocks were like those found on the surface of the Earth and they were roughly the same age as the Earth rocks. Scientists believe it is possible that the Moon was once part of the Earth. The only way enough rock from Earth could be flung into space to make the Moon was if something big – such as a planet the size of Mars – had hit the Earth very hard.

Rocks collected by astronauts show how the Moon formed.

Thousands of years ago the Moon looked bigger than it does today.

Spotlight on
space

The Moon is slowing down the Earth's spinning and our days are growing longer. When the Moon formed, a day was only six hours long. Today, a day is 24 hours long. Every 500 years, our day grows longer by one second.

Waxing and waning

The Moon seems to change shape from day to day. Some nights it looks like a bright ball in the sky, sometimes it is a half circle, or at other times a thin curve called a **crescent**. These different shapes happen every month and are called the phases of the Moon.

A trick of the light

The Moon does not really change shape. Every night it moves a little further around the Earth and we see more of its sunlit side until the whole face of the Moon is bright. Then, as the Moon continues on its journey around the Earth, we see less and less of the sunlit part each night.

Spotlight on space

When the Moon seems to be growing bigger, it is said to be waxing. After the full Moon, when it seems to grow small again, it is waning. There are 29 days between one full Moon and the next.

We see more and more of the Moon lit up each night until, at full Moon, the whole Moon is lit up.

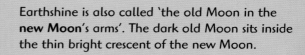

Earthshine is also called 'the old Moon in the **new Moon**'s arms'. The dark old Moon sits inside the thin bright crescent of the new Moon.

Earthshine

The dark part of the Moon is not always completely black. Sometimes, sunlight bounces off the Earth on to the Moon and gives it a faint glow. This is called **Earthshine**. The amount of sunlight that bounces off the Earth depends on what is on the sunlit side of the Earth. The sea reflects the least amount of light, clouds reflect the most. Measuring the brightness of Earthshine on the Moon tells scientists about how much cloud covers the Earth.

Naming the Moon

In different parts of the world, some people give the full Moon a new name each month.

Month		Name
January	▶	Wolf Moon
February	▶	Snow Moon
March	▶	Worm Moon
April	▶	Pink Moon
May	▶	Flower Moon
June	▶	Strawberry Moon
July	▶	Hay Moon
August	▶	Grain Moon
September	▶	Harvest Moon
October	▶	Hunter's Moon
November	▶	Frosty Moon
December	▶	Cold Moon

At the edge of the sunlit half of the Moon you can see the craters more clearly.

Moon studies

Scientists have been fascinated by the night sky for many thousands of years. They studied the movement of the stars and the Moon and made maps of what they saw. When the telescope was invented in the 1600s scientists could see the Moon in more detail than ever before. Telescopes make things look larger and nearer.

Bigger and better

There are two types of telescope. These are refractors and reflectors. A refractor uses a lens to form an image. A reflector uses a curved mirror instead of a lens to show the image. You can also use binoculars to look at the Moon. Binoculars are just like two small telescopes joined together.

You can use a telescope at home to see the Moon in more detail.

Powerful telescopes

Astronomers use very powerful telescopes on Earth and in space to study the Moon. Telescopes above the clouds and swirling air of the Earth's atmosphere have a clearer view of the Moon. They do not just make pictures of the Moon, they focus moonlight on to instruments that measure the different colours of light it contains. They also measure invisible rays, such as heat, coming from the Moon's surface. They measure the Moon's gravity too, and they search for gases leaking from its soil.

Bigger and stronger telescopes mean scientists can see the Moon's surface better than ever before. They can see mountains and craters.

Spotlight on
space

Different types of rock and soil reflect light in different ways. Instruments look for tiny variations in the way light bounces off the Moon and use them to make maps of the rocks and soil.

Colours have been added to this photograph of the Moon to show how many types of rock and soil are on the Moon's surface.

Rock and dust

The surface of the Moon is covered with shallow bowl shapes of all sizes. These are called craters. Craters are places where rocks from space have crashed into the Moon. Billions of years of being hit by rocks has smashed the Moon's surface into rocks and dust.

Making craters

A crater forms on the Moon when a rock hits it. The rock is smashed to bits and as it makes a hole in the surface of the Moon rock and dust is pushed up to create the walls of the crater.

This large crater is called Copernicus. It was named after the Polish astronomer Nicolaus Copernicus who was born in 1473.

Size of the Moon's craters

Archimedes	▶	82 kilometres across
Clavius	▶	225 kilometres across
Copernicus	▶	92 kilometres across
Kepler	▶	35 kilometres across
Plato	▶	97 kilometres across
Ptolemaeus	▶	148 kilometres across
Tycho	▶	87 kilometres across

The Moon's dark seas formed when giant rocks from space smashed into the Moon. **Lava** flooded up through the cracked crust and covered the surface.

Tycho is a **ray crater**. Bright rays spreading out on top of the dark surface show that it is a young crater.

Peaks and streaks

Craters bigger than 25 kilometres across often have a mountain peak in the middle. When a big rock crashes into the Moon, it hits so hard that it pushes the surface downwards. Then the surface bounces back and throws up the mountain in the middle. Some of the Moon's craters have bright streaks stretching away from them. The streaks are called rays. They are made from light-coloured dust thrown out when the crater was formed.

Spotlight on
space

One of the biggest lunar craters we can see from Earth is called Clavius. Just out of sight on the far side of the Moon, there is a much bigger crater called Mare Orientale. It is about 965 kilometres across.

The far side

The side of the Moon we never see is called the far side, or the dark side, of the Moon. No one knew what the far side of the Moon was like until the *Luna 3* **space probe** photographed it in 1959.

Mapping the Moon

In 1994, the *Clementine* **spacecraft** spent two months photographing the Moon. The photographs and measurements were used to make maps. But *Clementine*'s mission ended earlier than planned, when it spun out of control.

Clementine mission

Launched	▶	25 January 1994
Launched by	▶	*Titan* rocket
Spacecraft mass	▶	227 kilograms
Height	▶	1.9 metres
Size across the middle	▶	1.1 metres
Mission ended	▶	June 1994

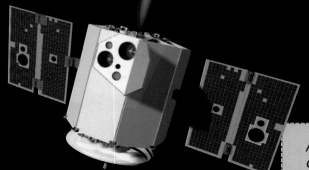

As well as photographing the Moon, *Clementine* made a very accurate map of the shape of the surface.

This crater on the far side of the Moon is full of lava. The crater is named after the Russian space scientist, Konstantin Tsiolkovsky.

Craters on the side of the Moon we can see are named after famous astronomers and scientists from history. Many of the craters on the far side of the Moon are named after more recent people.

The dark side of the Moon

Astronauts have not landed on the far side of the Moon yet, because they would be cut off from Earth. The USA plans to put communications satellites in orbit around the Moon, so that future astronauts on the far side will be able to talk to people on Earth. Astronomers are hoping to build **radio telescopes** on the far side of the Moon which make images from radio waves instead of light. On the far side of the Moon, the telescopes would not pick up unwanted radio waves from Earth.

The far side of the Moon is full of craters.

Visiting the Moon

More than 70 space missions have visited the Moon.
Most of them were small space probes. *Luna 2* was
the first. It crash landed on the Moon in 1959.
Since then, dozens of space probes have orbited
the Moon and landed on it.

Moon ice

The *Lunar Prospector* probe was sent to the Moon in 1998.
One of its jobs was to look for ice in craters at the Moon's
North **Pole** and South Pole. Craters there are always in shadow
and so ice in them stays frozen forever. The *Lunar Prospector*
did find ice in these craters.

Lunar Prospector was a tiny
space probe, only 1.4 metres
across and 1.3 metres high.

Spotlight on space

Space probes prepared
the way for people to go
to the Moon. They took
thousands of photographs
of places where astronauts
could land. They also tested
the surface to make sure
it was strong enough to
take the weight of
a spacecraft.

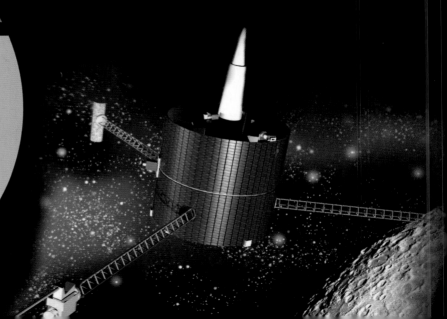

Cargo craft

Lunar Prospector carried a strange cargo to the Moon. It contained some of the **ashes** of a scientist called Dr Eugene Shoemaker who died in 1997. He was an expert on Moon rocks and had hoped to go to the Moon one day. At the end of its mission, *Lunar Prospector* was crashed into the Moon with the ashes. Scientists hoped the crash might melt some ice and throw water out into space, but none was seen.

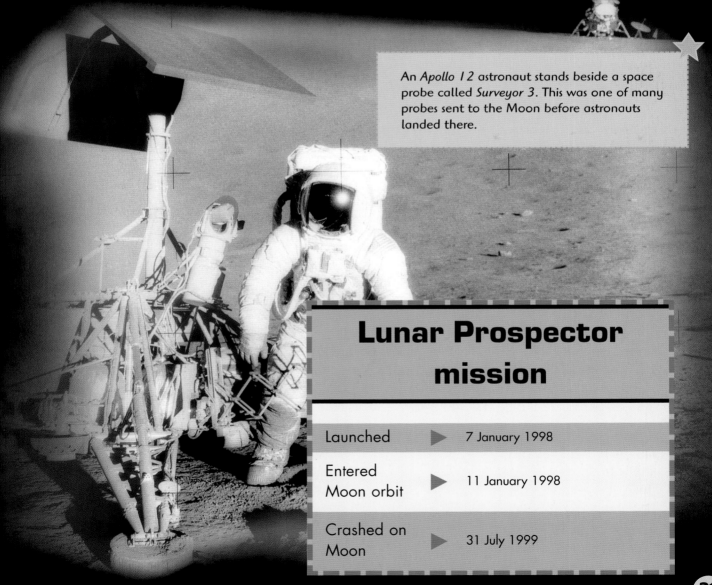

An *Apollo 12* astronaut stands beside a space probe called *Surveyor 3*. This was one of many probes sent to the Moon before astronauts landed there.

Lunar Prospector mission

Launched	▶	7 January 1998
Entered Moon orbit	▶	11 January 1998
Crashed on Moon	▶	31 July 1999

Moon walks

In the summer of 1969, a strange spider-like spacecraft touched down on the Moon. Inside, Neil Armstrong and Edwin 'Buzz' Aldrin became the first space explorers ever to land on the Moon. Soon afterwards, Armstrong stepped on to the Moon's surface, followed by Aldrin.

First steps on the Moon

Armstrong and Aldrin spent more than two hours walking about on the Moon. They collected nearly 22 kilograms of rocks and set up scientific experiments. A third astronaut, Michael Collins, orbited the Moon in another part of the *Apollo 11* spacecraft.

Half a billion people around the world watched the television pictures of 'Buzz' Aldrin walking on the Moon.

Apollo 11 mission

Launched	▶	16 July 1969
Landed	▶	20 July 1969
Launched from Moon	▶	21 July 1969
Returned to Earth	▶	24 July 1969

Apollo missions

Between 1969 and 1972, six *Apollo* missions landed 12 astronauts on the Moon. Between them they brought back 379 kilograms of Moon rocks to Earth for scientists to study. Only one of the Moon landing missions went wrong. While *Apollo 13* was on its way to the Moon, 330,000 kilometres away from Earth, there was an explosion inside the spacecraft. Scientists and engineers on Earth worked with the astronauts and helped them to bring their damaged spacecraft home safely.

An astronaut's footprint is stamped into the fine dust on the Moon's surface.

Spotlight on
space

Astronauts left lots of footprints on the Moon. On Earth they would be blown away by wind and washed away in the rain. But because there is no weather on the Moon, the footprints will be there millions of years from now.

The only scientist to go the Moon is Harrison Schmitt. He is a **geologist** – a rock expert. He was a member of the crew of *Apollo 17*.

Eclipses

As the Moon orbits the Earth and the Earth orbits the Sun, all three of them sometimes line up together in a row. If the Earth comes between the Sun and Moon, it casts a shadow on the Moon. This event is called a **lunar eclipse**.

Shadows

A total lunar eclipse happens when the whole Moon is darkened by the Earth's shadow. Sometimes only part of the Moon goes through the Earth's shadow so only part of the Moon goes dark. This is called a partial lunar eclipse.

Total lunar eclipses 2007 – 2010

Date		Seen from
3 March 2007	▶	USA, Europe, Africa, Asia
28 August 2007	▶	East Asia, Australia, Pacific, USA
11 July 2010	▶	Central Pacific, USA, Europe, Africa
21 December 2010	▶	East Asia, Australia, Pacific, USA, Europe

The curved edge of the Earth's shadow, seen on the Moon during a partial eclipse, shows the round shape of the Earth.

Spotlight on
space

Sometimes the Moon turns a beautiful red or orange colour during an eclipse.

Flat or round?

People in the ancient world did not know what shape the Earth was. Some people thought it was round, others said it was flat, because the ground seemed flat and they thought everything on the bottom of a round world would fall off. Then, about 2,350 years ago, a Greek philosopher called Aristotle saw that the Earth's shadow on the Moon was round. He wondered if this meant that the Earth was round. He was right.

The future

No one has been to the Moon since 1972. Now the USA is planning to send astronauts back to the Moon by 2020. In future the Moon may be used as a launch-pad to send astronauts to the planet Mars for the first time.

New spaceships

Astronauts will return to the Moon in a brand new fleet of spacecraft. A crew exploration vehicle will take them into orbit around the Moon. Then a **lander** vehicle will carry four astronauts to land on the Moon's surface. New style rockets and cargo spacecraft are also being built.

Spotlight on
space

The new crew exploration vehicle that will take astronauts to the Moon will be about two and half times the size of the Apollo spacecraft. It will be used later for manned missions to Mars.

A rocket of the future soars into space. Its nose cover falls away. Inside, a lunar landing craft is ready for its flight to the Moon.

Moon bases

By the year 2020, astronauts could be staying on the Moon for up to seven days at a time. At least two flights to the Moon every year are planned. All the supplies, equipment and spacecraft that are sent to the Moon could be used to build a permanent Moon base where astronauts could live for up to six months, learning how to live on another world.

Future astronauts will orbit the Moon in a new type of spacecraft.

Crew exploration vehicle facts

Height	▶	3.6 metres
Diameter	▶	5.5 metres
Weight	▶	9.5 tonnes
Crew	▶	up to 6
Can be used	▶	10 times

Timeline

150 BC
Greek astronomer Hipparchus makes the first accurate measurements of the size of the Moon and its distance from Earth.

1609
English astronomer Thomas Harriot is thought to be the first person to have looked at the Moon through a new invention, the telescope.

1610
Italian scientist Galileo Galilei publishes drawings of the Moon as he sees them through a telescope.

1647
Polish astronomer Johannes Hevelius draws an accurate map of the Moon.

1651
Italian Giovanni Battista Riccioli draws a map of the Moon with names for craters that we still use today.

1665
English scientist Robert Hooke does experiments to find out how craters formed.

1776
The first detailed map of the Moon is drawn by the German astronomer Johann Tobias Mayer.

1840
The first clear photograph of the Moon is taken by American John William Draper.

1909
German astronomer Philip Fauth publishes a book saying that there are glaciers (rivers of solid ice) on the Moon.

1959
Luna 1 is launched towards the Moon, but misses its target by a huge 6,000 kilometres.

The *Luna 2* space probe crashes on to the surface of the Moon.

The *Luna 3* space probe takes the first photographs of the far side of the Moon. For the first time, people see photos of what was known as 'the dark side of the moon'.

1964
The *Ranger 7* space probe takes the first close-up photographs of the Moon, before crashing on to it.

1965
Ranger 8 takes close-up photographs of the Sea of Tranquillity. The first astronauts land here four years later.

1966
The *Luna 9* space probe is the first to make a soft landing on the Moon, in the Ocean of Storms.

Luna 10 is the first space probe to orbit the Moon.

Surveyor 1 makes a soft landing on the Moon, in the Ocean of Storms. It sends 11,150 photographs back to Earth.

Lunar Orbiter 1 photographs parts of the Moon where astronauts will land.

1967
The *Surveyor 3* space probe lands on the Moon and digs a trench in its soil.

Surveyor 5 lands on the Moon and carries out the first chemical tests on the soil of another planet.

Surveyor 6 becomes the first spacecraft to take off from the Moon – it fires its rocket to make a short hop and land again just 2.4 metres away.

1968
Apollo 8 is the first space flight to carry astronauts around the Moon and back to Earth. This is the first time a human has seen the 'dark side of the moon' with his own eyes.

1969
Apollo 9 tests the lunar excursion module, the Moon-landing spacecraft, in Earth's orbit.

Apollo 10 flies to within 14 kilometres of the surface of the Moon.

Apollo 11 lands the first astronauts on the Moon. It is a historic day in space travel.

Apollo 12 lands astronauts on the Moon within walking distance of the *Surveyor 3* space probe.

1970
Luna 16 lands on the Moon, digs some soil out of the surface and takes off again, bringing the lunar soil back to Earth.

Apollo 13 is unable to land on the Moon because of an explosion in the spacecraft.

Luna 17 lands a rover called *Lunokhod 1* on the Moon. The rover travels more than 10.5 kilometres in 11 months and during this time takes thousands of photographs and tests the Moon's soil.

1971
Apollo 14 and *15* land astronauts on the Moon. *Apollo 15* takes an electric car called a lunar rover to the Moon.

1972
Apollo 16 lands astronauts on the Moon with a lunar rover.

Apollo 17 is the last manned Moon landing of the 20th century. Like *Apollo 15* and *16*, it carries a lunar rover.

1973
Luna 21 lands the *Lunokhod 2* rover on the Moon. It travels 37 kilometres and takes 80,000 photographs of the surface.

1994
The *Clementine* space probe maps the whole Moon.

1998
The *Lunar Prospector* space probe discovers ice in craters at the Moon's poles.

2020
Astronauts are due to return to the Moon.

Glossary

ashes The remains of a person's body that has been cremated or burnt instead of being buried.

astronauts People who travel through space.

astronomers Scientists who study the stars, planets and moons.

atmosphere The gas around a planet or moon. The Earth's atmosphere is made of air.

core Centre; the Moon's core is its centre.

craters Shallow round dips in the Moon's surface caused by a space rock smashing into it.

crescent One of the phases of the Moon, when only the thin curve of the edge of the Moon is lit up by the Sun.

crust The thin outer layer of the Moon.

Earthshine The glow on the dark side of the Moon caused by light reflected from the Earth.

full Moon One of the phases of the Moon, when the whole face of the Moon is lit up by the Sun.

geologist A person who studies the history of the Earth and its life, especially by studying its rocks.

gravity An invisible force that pulls things towards each other. Earth's gravity pulls us down on to the ground and keeps the Moon in orbit around the Earth.

lander A spacecraft designed to land on other planets.

lava Molten (liquid) rock thrown out by a volcano during an eruption.

legends Ancient stories passed on from one generation to the next, often orally.

lunar Anything to do with the Moon.

lunar eclipse An eclipse of the Moon; when the Moon goes dark as it passes through the Earth's shadow.

mantle The middle layer around the Moon between the core and the crust.

mass The more mass something has, the heavier it is.

moon A small object orbiting a planet. The Earth has one moon, called the Moon.

new Moon One of the phases of the Moon, when the whole face of the Moon is in darkness.

Norse myths Ancient stories from Scandinavia.

orbit To follow a path around the Sun.

planets Large objects in orbit around a star.

pole One of the furthest points at the north and south of a planet or moon.

radio telescopes Huge saucer-shaped dishes which collect radio waves instead of light waves.

ray crater A new crater with rays or streaks of rock and dust thrown out around it.

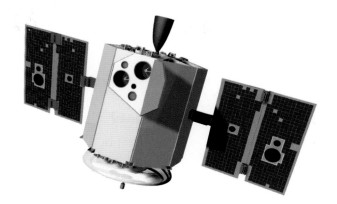

Solar System The Sun, planets, moons and everything else that orbits the Sun.

spacecraft A machine sent into space. Manned spacecraft have people inside. Unmanned spacecraft are controlled by computers.

space probe An unmanned spacecraft sent from Earth to explore space.

tides The rising and falling of the sea twice a day, caused by the pull of the Moon's gravity.

waning Becoming smaller. When the Moon is waning the bright, sunlit part becomes smaller each night.

waxing Becoming bigger. The Moon is waxing when the bright, sunlit part becomes bigger every night.

Index

Apollo 21, 22, 23, 26, 29
astronaut 5, 10, 19, 21, 22, 23, 26
astronomers 9, 15, 19

core 10
craters 4, 13, 15, 16, 17, 19, 20, 28, 29
crescent 12, 13

Earthshine 13
exploration vehicle 26, 27

geologist 23
glaciers 28
gravity 7, 10, 15

lava 17, 19
Luna 18, 20, 28, 29
lunar 17, 20, 21, 24, 26, 28, 29
lunar eclipse 24
Lunar Orbiter 28
Lunar Prospector 20, 21, 29
Lunokhod 2 29

mantle 10
mission 18, 21, 22

partial eclipse 24
probe 18, 20, 21, 28, 29

Ranger 28

rockets 18, 26
rover 29

spacecraft 18, 20, 22, 23, 26, 27, 29
sunlight 5, 13, 25
Surveyor 21, 28, 29

telescope 14, 15, 19, 28
tides 7
trench 28

waning 12
waxing 12
werewolves 8

WEBFINDER

http://www.bbc.co.uk/science/space/solarsystem/earth/moon.shtml

http://starchild.gsfc.nasa.gov/docs/StarChild/solar_system_level1/moon.html

http://www.astronomytoday.com/astronomy/moon.html

http://kids.nineplanets.org/moon.htm

http://www.moonpeople.com/html/kids/kids.html

http://astronomy.com/asy/default.aspx?c=a&id=1219

http://www.kidsastronomy.com/earth/moons.htm

http://archives.cbc.ca/IDC-1-69-1587-10802/life_society/60s/clip12

http://www.dustbunny.com/afk/planets/earth/moon.html